EVALUATING INFORMATION

Beth A. Pulver and Donald C. Adcock

Heinemann
LIBRARY

www.heinemann.co.uk/library

Visit our website to find out more information about Heinemann Library books.

To order:

☎ Phone 44 (0) 1865 888066

📄 Send a fax to 44 (0) 1865 314091

💻 Visit the Raintree bookshop at www.heinemann.co.uk/library to browse our catalogue and order online.

Heinemann Library is an imprint of **Pearson Education Limited**, a company incorporated in England and Wales having its registered office at Edinburgh Gate, Harlow, Essex, CM20 2JE – Registered company number: 00872828

Heinemann is a registered trademark of Pearson Education Ltd.

Edited by Andrew Farrow and Marta Segal Block
Designed by Richard Parker and Tinstar Design Ltd.
Picture research by Fiona Orbell and
    Elizabeth Alexander
Production: Alison Parsons

Originated by Chroma Graphics (Overseas) Pte. Ltd
Printed and bound in China by Leo Paper Group.

ISBN 978 0 431 90817 5 (hardback)
13 12 11 10 09
10 9 8 7 6 5 4 3 2

British Library Cataloguing in Publication Data

Pulver, Beth A.
  Evaluating information. - (Information literacy skills)
  028.7

A full catalogue record for this book is available from the British Library.

Acknowledgements

The author and publishers are grateful to the following for permission to reproduce copyright material: © 2008 Google p. 31; © Corbis pp. /Gabe Palmer **4, 40**, /MAPS.com **11** (bottom), /moodboard **45**, /Neil Farrin/JAI **6** (left), /Ron Sachs/CNP **16**; © Corbi/Barbara Walton/epa p. **20**; © Courtesy of The University of Texas Libraries, The University of Texas at Austin p. **11** (top); © Digital Vision p. **7**; © Getty Images pp. /Reza Estakhrian **23**, /Time & Life Pictures **27**; Newsweek, (February 25) © 2008, Newsweek Inc. All rights reserved. Used by permission and protected by the Copyright Laws of the United States. The printing, copying, redistribution or retransmission of the Material without express written permission is prohibited p. **28**; © Image courtesy of PETA p. **21**; © PA photos/AP p. **28**; © iStockphoto pp. /Kirsty Pargeter **12**, /Vivek Nigam **14**; © KPT Power Photos p. **6** (right); © Royal Society for the Protection of Birds (RSPB) p. **15**; © The OLPC WIWI p. **33**.

Background features and cover photograph reproduced with permission of © iStockphoto.

Every effort has been made to contact copyright holders of any material reproduced in this book. Any omissions will be rectified in subsequent printings if notice is given to the publishers.

Disclaimer

Contents

Some words are shown in bold, **like this.** You can find the definitions for these words in the glossary.

The Basics of Evaluation

You receive information every day, and you evaluate that information, often without even thinking about it. Imagine you are watching the news on TV. The weather person tells you that tomorrow it will be sunny and warm. You believe her. After the weather, a sports commentator interviews a football coach who says that your favourite team has no way of making it to the finals. The coach works for a rival team. You know that some of what he says is true, but you also know that he doesn't want your team to win, so you take this into account. Then there's an advert. It tells you that the way to become more popular is to buy lipstick. You know the advert is trying to sell you lipstick, so you don't believe it at all. You've made all these decisions about what is fact and what is **opinion** without even thinking about it. You already know how to evaluate information.

Definition of evaluate

To determine the significance, worth, or condition of, usually by careful appraisal and study.

You can get information from books, newspapers, television, CDs, magazines, and the Internet, but how do you know if the information is relevant, accurate, or complete enough to answer your question?

The same is true for information you find when you do research. You need to learn how to evaluate it. You should be able to tell when something is trustworthy, when a source shows a **bias** (or preference), and the difference between fact and opinion. You must also learn how to decide when you have enough information.

This book will discuss how to evaluate information to determine if it is relevant, accurate, and complete. You will also learn how to evaluate opinions, and how to include opinions in your research.

The 5 Ws

Evaluating information is an important part of the research process. One tool you can use in evaluating information is the 5 Ws. Answering each of the 5 W questions – who, what, when, where, and why – will help you determine if the information is useful in answering your question or solving your problem. The questions test the accuracy and relevance of the information.

The 5 Ws

Who
- Who is the author?
- Is the author an expert?
- Is there a biography of the author included?

What
- What does the author say is the purpose of his/her writing?
- What else might the author have in mind for this writing?

When
- When was the work written?
- Is the currency of the information important in answering your research question?

Where
- Where did the information come from?
- Is the information biased in anyway?
- Does the information include inaccurate or misleading material?

Why
- Why is this information useful in answering your question?
- Why is this source better than others you have looked at?

Relevance, Accuracy, & Completeness

Relevance: Does the information meet my needs?

In researching your topic, you will consult many resources and read many facts. Some of the facts will be related to, but not relevant to, your topic. By relevant, we mean that they can help you answer your question. In evaluating the information, you need to decide if the information is both related to and relevant to the question you are trying to answer. If the information is related to your topic, is it important enough to include in your research? If the answer is yes, you will be closer to answering your question or solving your problem.

If you were researching kiwis, you might find important information on both of these. The information on the bird might be related to the fruit, but it would not be relevant.

When you first start a research project, you may not know which information is relevant and which is not. The clearer you are about your research topic, the easier it will be to work this out. Collecting irrelevant information can make it more difficult to answer your question. Be sure to give yourself plenty of time to conduct your research, so you can collect and discard information that is not relevant.

Determining relevant information

Let's look at an example of determining relevant information. A pupil is researching the causes of global warming. The pupil finds this piece of information in a book on global warming:

"Progress in science depends on the continual testing of results and explanations. Such skepticism makes it highly unlikely that scientists will ever unanimously recommend a solution . . . ." (Taken from: Philander, S. George. *Is the Temperature Rising?* Princeton, NJ: Princeton University Press, 1998, p. 9.)

The pupil must examine the statement to decide if it is related to the topic "The Causes of Global Warming". As they read the statement, they must ask the question: Does this information discuss the causes of global warming? After careful examination, the pupil decides that the statement does discuss how scientists solve problems such as global warming. The pupil decides that, although this information is *related* to the topic of global warming, it is not *relevant* to their research question. The pupil decides not to use this fact, because it does not provide an answer or give an example of a cause of global warming.

Is this evidence of global warming?

Accuracy: Is the information correct?

When you first started school, you were probably taught that things are either fact or fiction, true or false. Generally this is true. However, sometimes it isn't always clear if something is a fact. Facts can change over time. Two people can read the same information and come to two different conclusions. Part of your job as a researcher is to make sure the information you are using is accurate, so that you end up with the correct facts.

Multiple sources

Using more than one source is a good way to make sure you are finding accurate information. If you find the same piece of information in three or more sources, it is probably correct. Sometimes using more than one source can be confusing. What if you find three sources that say one thing, and three that say another? You will have to judge which sources to trust.

The author and consultants

One tool for judging a source is to consider who wrote it. Most books include information about the author, either on the back cover or somewhere inside the book. Magazine articles often give this information in a special "contributors" section that has information on all the authors in that issue. Other sources, such as encyclopedias and dictionaries, may not list individual writers. For these sources you have to decide if the publishing company itself is trustworthy. Many publishing companies use experts and other consultants to check that the information in their books and magazines is accurate. These consultants are often listed in the book or on the back cover.

Internet sources

Judging whether or not an Internet source is reliable can be especially difficult. The Uniform Resource Locator (**URL),** or Web address, can help you decide if a website is worth using. The URL is divided into three parts. The first part (www) tells you that it is an address on the World Wide Web. The next part is the name or title of the Web page. The final part is the **domain name**. This tells you what kind of a website it is. The most common domain names are companies, educational institutions, organizations, and governments.

Parts of a Web address

http://www.un.org/

http = Hyper Text Transfer Protocol
Helps your computer find the web page.

www = World Wide Web
Means that the page is on the World Wide Web.

un = United Nations
This is the name of the organization, company, or person that the website belongs to.

org = domain name
This tells you what kind of website it is.

Domain names

.com = commercial site

.gov = governmental site

.org = organization

.ac = university

.net = network service provider, Internet administrative site

International sites will end in an abbreviation for the country, such as ".uk" for United Kingdom.

Who wrote it?

Trying to find out who writes or publishes a website can be tricky, as it may not be obvious. Information can be posted online anonymously or with a false name. Some websites contain an "about us" page, which may give details of who sponsors and writes the site. If you cannot find enough information about a website, it is best not to include it as a source.

Is the information current?

One way of checking that a source is reliable is to make sure it is current. You will need to make sure the information is up-to-date. Check when the source was created. In books look for the **copyright date**. In magazines and newspapers look for the date they were published. On websites and **databases** look for the date they were created or posted to the Internet. Sometimes this will be a copyright date. Other electronic sources, such as videos, DVDs, or CDs, will display a copyright date on their packaging and sometimes on the video or disc label.

Let's look at an example of why dates are so important. Imagine a pupil is doing a project on Russia. They find an atlas from 1990. Russia looked very different in 1990, before the collapse of the Soviet Union and the formation of many other countries. If the pupil used this old map, their project would not be accurate.

Completeness: Do I have enough information?

As you research the answer to your question or solution to your problem, it can be difficult to know if you have enough information. Each information source you use must provide you with facts you need to answer the research question or solve the problem. You must examine the information you have found to determine how complete it is. Sometimes you will find facts that are accurate and relevant, but do not provide enough information to answer your question or solve your problem. In this case you will have to find more resources.

Finding enough facts that go together can be like finding all the pieces of a jigsaw puzzle. It can take a lot of patient research, but it's rewarding in the end.

These two maps show why dates are important. If a pupil used
the old map of the Soviet Union (above), before it collapsed in
1990, the research would not be accurate.

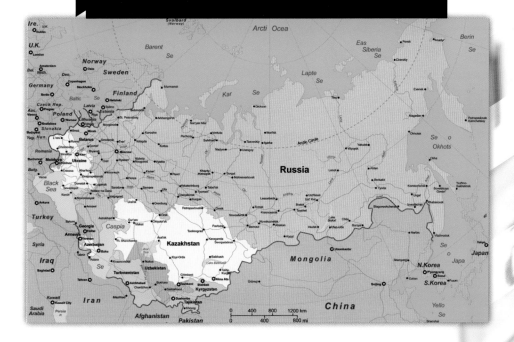

Rough drafts

One way to work out if you have enough information is to begin writing a **rough draft** of your project. As you do this, you will start to see where you have gaps and need more research. Having an organized draft will make these gaps clearer. It's a good idea to organize your paper into three parts: an introductory statement or **topic sentence**, supporting detail statements, and a conclusion. Whether you have one paragraph or many, your essay will probably follow this format.

Do you have enough information? Organizing your material carefully will help you complete the research puzzle.

For a long essay, you will have an introductory paragraph, several paragraphs of information that supports your introduction, and a concluding paragraph that summarizes the content of your essay. As you finish your rough draft, you will know if you have enough information to answer your question or solve your problem.

How many drafts?

At school, your teacher may tell you how many drafts of your essay you should write. They may also teach you note-taking techniques and drafting skills. At school, and for the rest of your life, you will have to come up with a system that works for you. For now you should follow the methods outlined by your teacher. This will help you to develop your study skills.

Model of the research process

Question to be answered or problem to be solved		
Supporting sentence or details	Supporting sentence or details	Supporting sentence or details
Answer to the question or solution to the problem		

Facts, Opinions, & Points of View

A fact is a piece of information that is known to be true. Most facts are easy to **verify**. Here are some examples of facts: the capital of Hungary is Budapest, water freezes at 32° Fahrenheit (0° Celsius), and World War I started in 1914.

These facts are considered **common knowledge**, and are easy to verify in any source. As you are doing research to answer your question or solve your problem, there will be facts that you already know about your topic. But there are other facts you will need to find and verify with supporting information. You can verify them by using several sources. Some facts are less easy to verify than these examples. Being able to find information and evaluate if it is true, false, or needs more support is a valuable skill.

Water freezes at 32°F (0°C). This sort of fact only needs to be confirmed by one source.

Opinions

We all have opinions. Some opinions are what is known as a matter of taste. For example, you may have a favourite colour or a food you don't like. It is almost impossible to argue about these things. It is also almost impossible for research to change your mind. If you don't like chocolate, no amount of research is going to change that.

Sometimes when you do research you come across people's opinions. These can be difficult to recognize, because the author may use facts to support his or her opinion. If you agree with an opinion, you might think it is more fact than opinion. This is why trustworthy sources make it clear when an article is a factual article or an opinion piece. Newspapers often include opinion pieces. These may contain facts, but their purpose is primarily to give the opinion of the writer. This is different from a news article from elsewhere in the paper.

ADVERTISING PROMOTION

The RSPB is at the forefront of campaigns to save wildlife and the natural habitats it depends on. Here are just some of its campaign success stories

SAVING NATURE

Wildlife is, for many reasons in our modern world, constantly under threat. Yet there is an organisation that makes it its business to speak out for birds and wildlife, take action and help keep our natural world safe. When a new airport development was proposed in 2002 at Cliffe in the marshes of Kent — threatening a vital habitat for wetland birds, water voles and endangered insects — the environmental charity launched a campaign that saw 150,000 of its members petitioning the government to oppose the development. Letters were also written to the government and a lobby in Westminster put members face to face with their MPs. It worked: in 2003 the Cliffe airport proposal was dropped.

THE RSPB IS SAVING SPECIES ACROSS THE GLOBE

Sometimes advertisers make it difficult to tell the difference between their advertisement and a news article.

Points of view

You may have learned about the point of view of an author when studying literature. In fiction, the perspective, or point of view, of the author is called their voice. Authors are allowed to include their point of view or bias as a part of the writing of fiction. But in reference materials, they are expected to present only facts. Some non-fiction works are meant to express an opinion. This is fine, but when you are doing research, you should be able to tell if the work is meant to be unbiased or an opinion piece.

Showing bias

Sometimes when you hold a strong opinion it can influence the way you view and write about facts. Bias is when an author's point of view influences his or her writing. The author might be trying to influence the reader, or their bias may simply affect how they honestly view the situation. Bias can be subtle and difficult to spot. It can be presented as fact, when it is really the author's opinion. Or it may be obvious. Politicians use biased information in their campaigns to influence voters to elect them.

Are these the best people to ask about their candidate's record, or are their opinions likely to be biased?

You come across bias in information sources every day. For example, you would expect an advertisement to be biased, because it is selling a product. There are other sources, however, that may seem **objective**, or impartial, but have a reason to be biased. One such example is **technical reports**. These reports are based on the research of a scientific experiment or study. They are often funded by groups that have an interest in the outcome of the research. For example, a drug company may sponsor experiments to see if a drug is effective or safe. The fact that a company with an interest in the outcome paid for the research does not automatically mean the outcome is invalid, but any information in the researchers' reports should be confirmed by an independent, objective source.

Sometimes people can get carried away in discounting any information that comes from a source with a point of view. The fact that someone has a bias does not necessarily mean they are wrong. It simply means that you should be aware of it when evaluating the information.

Common examples of bias

Advertisements
Contain bias because they are selling a product. Sometimes advertisements are disguised as articles.

Political statements
Contain bias because they are trying to convince others of an opinion.

Scientific research
Although science is supposed to be objective, the results of experiments can be influenced by the researcher's opinions.

Using Facts, Opinions, & Points of View

When researching a question or looking for a solution to a problem, you will look for facts. You may use opinions as quotes within your writing, to add support to the facts you have found. In looking for answers to research questions or solutions to problems, you will want to avoid bias and opinions. There may be times, however, when your research question may require you to look at biased information and opinions.

Case study: Using animals in medical research

Take for example a pupil asked to research whether or not animals should be used for testing medical drugs and devices, and to choose a point of view on the subject. The pupil must adopt a position on the topic. Before they do this, they must undertake research. They must look at both sides of the issue, and be aware of bias and opinions. The pupil can use facts and opinions that support his or her point of view on the subject, and also those that counter the opposing point of view. They must use facts to support their position.

The panels on the opposite page show examples of how a pupil might list the issues, positions, and opinions relating to this topic.

The research

Before beginning research, the pupil must discover the issues involved in the topic. One way to do this is to review **blogs**. A blog is a website where people post opinions and have conversations. In the beginning, blogs were mainly kept by people as a sort of diary. Today many companies, organizations, and news sources pay people to keep blogs on certain topics. Like all sources, blogs need to be evaluated for accuracy. Looking at blogs can be a good way to get ideas about your topic. Typing "animal research blog" into a search engine will result in a lot of hits.

Examples, issues, positions, and opinions about animal testing

Issues in animal testing

- What are the issues surrounding the question?
- What countries have bans on animal testing, and what were the results of those bans?
- Are there any companies that have stopped doing animal testing?
- How would the ban affect medical research?
- What is the definition of medical research?
- What is the definition of animal testing?

Possible positions

- Allow all testing on animals.
- Outlaw all testing on animals.
- Allow testing only if there is no other option.
- Allow testing only after certain conditions have been met.
- Allow testing only if the drug or device saves lives.

Who will have an opinion?

- Drug companies
- Business groups
- Animal rights groups
- Medical professionals
- Political groups
- Individuals

Being aware of the biases surrounding an issue will help you to decide if information is strictly factual.

During an Internet search, the pupil might come across the website for PETA (see page 21). PETA stands for People for the Ethical Treatment of Animals. They believe that animals have rights and should not be used in medical ressearch. PETA says very clearly that they do not believe animals should be used in testing. This means that their bias is clear. When reading the information and sources PETA provides, a researcher needs to be aware of this bias.

In the United Kingdom, the BBC provides a source for relatively unbiased news. The BBC does not accept advertising. This means that advertisers such as medical companies cannot influence the news they provide. The BBC is a good source for discussions of controversial issues, because it tries to provide information from both sides. In a Web search, the pupil may come across a page from the BBC's website about a programme that included a debate. They could download a recording of that debate. Because the debate includes opinions on both sides of the issue, it is a good source of information.

Animal welfare is a subject that raises strong opinions on both sides of the debate.

Rules for discussing opinions

- Make sure you've done your research.
- Make sure you understand all the issues, not just the ones you care about.
- Don't bring in information that isn't relevant.
- Fight fair, don't make personal attacks.
- Listen to the other person's point of view.

PETA is an international organization concerned with animal rights. The information on their site may be biased, but that does not mean it is incorrect.

Inaccurate or Misleading Information

You can find correct, accurate information in a matter of seconds. However, you can also find incorrect and misleading information in that time. In the past, there were only a few sources of information: books, periodicals, newspapers, radio, and three or four TV channels.

Changes in technology mean that information sources have grown tremendously. Not only is there the Internet, there are also more books, magazines, and newspapers being published then ever before, and there are hundreds of TV channels. All these books, TV channels, websites, and magazines need information to publish and broadcast. This means that a lot of information is published or broadcast that may or may not be accurate.

In the past, if you wanted to write a book you had to find a publisher to publish it. This publisher would probably hire editors and fact checkers to make sure that what you were writing was correct. This means that by the time the book got to the library or bookshop, it had already been reviewed pretty carefully. Today, however, anyone with a computer can publish a book or put up a website. The information in the website does not have to be reviewed by anyone. One person can read it and pass the link on to other websites. Before you know it, one person's misleading statement is being reported as fact on hundreds of other websites.

While the old publishing system was good for ensuring accuracy, it also meant that only the information publishers wanted to publish was available. Publishing is a business. Publishers usually do not create a book unless they think it will sell well. The Internet allows a wider range of information and opinions to be available.

The fact that there is so much misleading information available makes it important for you to learn how to check the accuracy of your information. When writing an essay or stating an opinion, you are responsible for ensuring the accuracy of your information.

Changes in the publishing process may have resulted
in more inaccurate information being published.

Conflicting information

As you research the answer to your question or find the solution to your problem, you may find conflicting information. This means that some of the information you have found is inaccurate or misleading. There are several ways to determine which information is accurate.

Ways to determine accuracy

Who is the author or creator?
Is the information current?
Can the information be confirmed in more than one source?

The author

Determining the background of the author is mainly relevant when you think a piece is biased, or when you are dealing with opinions. Many reference books contain articles written by people who are not necessarily experts in the field, but who have researched the topic and reported it accurately. However, if you are trying to determine which of two conflicting sources is accurate, looking at the background of the authors may be helpful.

You can usually find information about the author in a book, magazine, newspaper, or electronic source. If it's not included, you will need to use other sources to find it. Publishers include information about the author at either the front or back of a book, or on the back cover. Magazine and newspaper articles usually state the qualifications of the author at the beginning or end of the article. It is more difficult to find information about the author on websites and other electronic resources.

Is the information current?

We tend to think of facts as things that don't change, but they do. Imagine a pupil studying the solar system. He finds an article about the planet Pluto dated 2005. The pupil writes an essay about the nine planets, with a focus on Pluto. The problem is, in 2006 scientists decided that Pluto does not actually meet the requirements for being a planet. Today there are officially only eight planets, and Pluto is not one of them. This means the pupil's entire essay would be wrong.

When old is good

You may wonder why libraries keep old, out-of-date books and magazines. Imagine you want to write an essay about life for people in the Soviet Union in the 1970s. As discussed earlier, this area of the world has changed a lot since the 1970s. You might want to read some magazine articles or encyclopedia entries from that period, to see what the views of the time were. People writing fiction might want to look at historical sources to create a believable world for the characters in their novels.

What do you think

Features of the series:

◆ Techniques for thinking critically and creatively

◆ A wealth of facts and opinions

◆ Ideas for organizing debates and discussions

Author Kate Shuster is Director of Debate Outreach at Claremont McKenna College in California. A former college U.S. National Debate Champion herself, Kate has coached five teams to national championships. As well as being the author of various textbooks on debate and public speaking, she now runs the largest secondary school debate outreach programme in the United States.

Consultant Dr- Geza Gyuk is Director of Astronomy at the Adler Planetarium in Chicago. He has research interests in asteroids, high-energy gamma-ray astronomy, and the search for life beyond Earth.

The title of this book is *What Do You Think?: Is There Other Life in the Universe?* It is about assessing ideas and evidence for extraterrestrial life. As you can see, the author and consultant are experts on these subjects.

Pluto is just one example of why it is important to know when a source was written or created. With a book you can use the copyright date, which is found on the **imprint page**. The copyright date tells you when the book was finished and published. The imprint page provides other helpful information. It tells you where the book was published and how to contact the publisher. It also tells you if the book is registered with the British Library.

www.heinemann.co.uk/library
Visit our website to find out more information about Heinemann Library books.

To order:
☎ Phone 44 (0) 1865 888066
🖹 Send a fax to 44 (0) 1865 314091
🖳 Visit the Raintree bookshop at www.heinemann.co.uk/library to browse our catalogue and order online.

Heinemann Library is an imprint of **Pearson Education Limited**, a company incorporated in England and Wales having its registered office at Edinburgh Gate, Harlow, Essex, CM20 2JE – Registered company number: 00872828

Heinemann is a registered trademark of Pearson Education Ltd.

Text © Pearson Education Limited 2008
First published in hardback in 2009
The moral rights of the proprietor have been asserted.

All rights reserved. No part of this publication may be reproduced in any form or by any means (including photocopying or storing it in any medium by electronic means and whether or not transiently or incidentally to some other use of this publication) without the written permission of the copyright owner, except in accordance with the provisions of the Copyright, Designs and Patents Act 1988 or under the terms of a licence issued by the Copyright Licensing Agency, Saffron House, 6–10 Kirby Street, London EC1N 8TS (www.cla.co.uk). Applications for the copyright owner's written permission should be addressed to the publisher.

Edited by Kristen Truhlar, Rachel Howells, and Louise Galpine
Designed by Richard Parker and Manhattan Design
Picture research by Mica Brancic
Production: Victoria Fitzgerald

Originated by Chroma Graphics (Overseas) Pte. Ltd
Printed and bound in China by Leo Paper Group.

ISBN 978 0 431 90804 5 (hardback)
13 12 11 10 09
10 9 8 7 6 5 4 3 2 1

British Library Cataloguing in Publication Data
Mattern, Joanne, 1963-
Bullying. - (The real deal)
155.9'2

A full catalogue record for this book is available from the British Library.

Acknowledgements
We would like to thank the following for permission to reproduce photographs: ©Alamy pp. 10 (Dennis MacDonald), 11 (Vario Images), 17 (Adrian Sherratt), 23 (David Levenson), 4, 27; ©Corbis pp. 6 (Martin Ruetschi/Keystone), 18 (Anthony Redpath), 16; ©Getty Images pp. 5 (Kevin Fitzgerald), 12, 20, 24 (Stone), 26 (Asia Images); ©Imagestate p. 13; ©Jupiter Images pp. 9 (BananaStock), 25 (Workbook Stock), 15; ©Photolibrary pp. 14 (Digital Vision), 19 (Creatas), 7; ©PunchStock pp. 8 (Jupiter), 22 (Tetra Images).

Cover photograph of a fist reproduced with permission of iStockphoto/Boris Yantov; cover photograph of teenager reproduced with permission of iStockphoto/Ivan Mateev.

We would like to thank Anne E. Pezalla for her invaluable help in the preparation of this book.

Every effort has been made to contact copyright holders of any material reproduced in this book. Any omissions will be rectified in subsequent printings if notice is given to the publishers.

Disclaimer
All the Internet addresses (URLs) given in this book were valid at the time of going to press. However, due to the dynamic nature of the Internet, some addresses may have changed, or sites may have changed or ceased to exist since publication. While the author and publishers regret any inconvenience this may cause readers, no responsibility for any such changes can be accepted by either the author or the publishers. It is recommended that adults supervise children on the Internet.

See if you can find the copyright date of this book. Then look inside the front of the book you are reading and find the same information.

The British Library is one of the biggest libraries in the world. All UK publishers must send a copy of every book they publish to the British Library. The books include the British Library's Cataloguing in Publication (CIP) data on their imprint page. This is the library's record of the book. If a book does not contain CIP data on its imprint page, it may have been published in another country, or by a small publisher, an organization, or the author. When CIP data is not included in a book, you need to verify the information.

In some books you will see that it is in a second, third, or even higher edition. This means that some of the information in the book has been rewritten or updated since the book was originally published. This happens most frequently with textbooks, reference books, and other non-fiction titles. When looking for books, make sure you have the most up-to-date edition available.

Dates of periodicals

Magazines, newspapers, and journals usually give the date listed on the cover or on the masthead. The masthead of a magazine is similar to the imprint page of a book. It lists the people involved in creating it. When using a database to find magazine articles, make sure the articles you find are up-to-date.

It is usually easy to find the publication date of a periodical.

Dates of websites

Websites and other electronic sources usually have a copyright date, or a date when the information was posted. Because website information can change so quickly, you need to keep track of not only the date the information was posted, but the date you found it. It may be that in between doing your research and your writing, a website changes its information or gets taken down. If this happens and you need more information, you will need to find a second source.

Sometimes it can be difficult to find a website's publication date, but it is important information.

How many sources?

Your teacher may specify how many sources your project should have. Many publishers require that every fact in a book be confirmed in at least two sources. If your teacher does not give you specific guidance, you will have to decide for yourself how many sources you need.

If a fact is considered common knowledge, such as the capital of a country, you only need to confirm it in one reliable source. Even if you are sure you know the fact, you should still confirm it. If a fact is less clear or open to debate, you should confirm it in at least two reliable sources. If you find conflicting facts, you may need to find a third or fourth source.

Conflicting sources

You may occasionally find a fact that is important to your research, but that you simply cannot verify in a second source. In this case you should be honest about the fact in your writing. You can use a statement such as, "Although it is unconfirmed, *Tiger Beat* magazine claims. . . ." Unconfirmed means that you found the fact, but cannot find a way to prove that it is true. When doing research, you should be careful if an article contains too many statements such as this.

Some facts, such as the population of a city or country, may be listed differently in equally reliable sources. This is because the sources have different ways of gathering such information. In this case it is acceptable to say, "The population of Chicago is approximately 3,000,000 people," or, "According to some sources, Chicago's population is 3,000,000; others list it slightly higher."

The most important thing is to be honest about where you found your information and what information you found. This allows your reader to form his or her own opinions.

Evaluating Websites

Because websites form such an important part of doing research today, and because there are so many of them, it is worth looking closely at how to evaluate them. The skills you use for evaluating other materials are all relevant to evaluating websites, just as the skills you use in evaluating websites are relevant to the rest of your research.

How the Internet is different

The Internet is unique, in that anyone can post information to it, with very little expense or time. Because it is so easy to post information to the Internet, there is masses of information on many topics. Some of this information is intended to inform you, some is to persuade you to agree with the author's position on an issue, and some is there to sell you something. Some information online is there with the specific purpose of tricking you, or conveying incorrect information.

Finding websites

The first step in finding a trustworthy website is to use a trustworthy source to find it. **Search engines** help you find websites. To use a search engine you type in a few **key words**, and within seconds the engine finds every website that uses those key words. The first few websites listed are the ones the search engine thinks are most relevant to your search.

This is obviously very helpful, but it can also be misleading or overwhelming. Many search engines run separate search engines for children. A popular example of this sort of search engine is www.askforkids.com. These search engines only look for information on a pre-approved list of websites. This can be helpful, because it means you are not getting **hits** that may be inappropriate for you. However, if you are researching a topic that is considered adult, these sites may not be able to help you.

Web directories

Another helpful resource can be a Web **directory**. A Web directory is a bit like a phone book. It does not contain every website, just websites the directory has chosen to include. Some directories choose their sites because they pay to be included. Others choose sites they approve of. Directories also provide separate directories for children. A popular example of this sort of directory is www.yahooligans.com. In either case, you should remember that the sites chosen may reflect the bias of the directory.

Web   Images   Maps   News   Shopping   Mail   more ▼

Google™

Pluto Planet

Search: ⦿ the web ◯ pages from the UK

Web   Results **1 - 10** of about **462,000** for Pluto Planet. **(0.31 seconds)**

Image results for **Pluto Planet**

  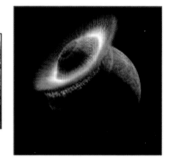

BBC NEWS | Science/Nature | Pluto loses status as a planet
Astronomers meeting in the Czech capital vote to strip **Pluto** of its status as a
call it a "dwarf **planet**".
news.bbc.co.uk/2/hi/in_depth/5282440.stm - 48k - Cached - Similar pages

Pluto Not a Planet, Astronomers Rule
24 Aug 2006 ... **Pluto** is no longer a **planet**, according to a new official definiti
icy sphere will be considered one of more than 40 "dwarf ...
news.nationalgeographic.com/ news/2006/08/060824-**pluto-planet**.html - 26k -
Cached - Similar pages

Pluto - Wikipedia, the free encyclopedia
Originally classified as a **planet**, **Pluto** is now considered the largest member

This shows you how many websites might contain
information about the former planet, Pluto.

Detecting reliability

For a website to be considered reliable, it should be clear who creates the site and why. Imagine for example that during a local election you are researching the candidates. If you came across the site www.libdems.org.uk, you would know that this was the website of the Liberal Democrat Party. You would know that the site was biased in favour of one candidate, but its bias would be clear. Other sites might not be as clear. If the name of the website does not clearly explain the purpose of the site, you should look for information about who created it on the site itself. If this information is not clearly available, the creator of the site may be trying to hide his or her biases, and the site may not be trustworthy.

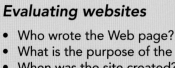

Evaluating websites

- Who wrote the Web page?
- What is the purpose of the Web page?
- When was the site created?
- When was the site last updated?
- Where does the information come from?
- Why is the information useful to you?
- Can the information be confirmed?

Wikis

You are probably familiar with Wikipedia. This is an online encyclopedia that readers can edit. It is probably the most famous example of **wiki** software. Wiki software allows groups and individuals to easily edit, create, and link pages together. It is used by companies and organizations that want their members to have access to the site. Some people consider wiki sites to be unreliable resources. When using a wiki site as a resource, you should try to find out if there are any rules for how changes are made. If you are unsure about a wiki site's reliability, you should try to find additional sources to back up the information you found.

Can unreliable sources be useful?

Research is a process. As you work on your essay or project, you will find information that is not relevant. You will also find information that is wrong or unreliable. This is part of the process. You should not use this information in your writing; however, it can still be useful. An unreliable source may give you a new idea, or it may point you in the right direction. It is OK to read unreliable sources. It is not OK to use them as your only sources.

one laptop per child

translate ▼

article · discussion · view source · history

The OLPC Wiki

english I عربي I български I deutsch I español I français I kreyòl ayisyen I italiano I 日本語 I 한국어 I монгол I ?????? I norsk I portu... I română I русский I kinyarwanda I türkçe I 中文 I 繁體中文

Welcome to the One Laptop per Child Wiki, a collaborative site about the OLPC project and related comm...
We are currently working on 5,784 pages in over twenty languages.

Learn More · Get Involved · What's New · About this wiki

The mission of the One Laptop per Child association is to develop a low-cost laptop—the "XO Laptop"—to revolutionize how we educate the world's children. Our goal is to provide children around the world with new opportunities to explore, experiment, and express themselves.

Why do children in developing nations need laptops? Laptops are a window and a tool: a window into the world and a tool with which to think. They are a wonderful way for all children to learn learning through independent interaction and exploration.

One Laptop per Child 🗗
transformation of educa...
who don't have the oppo...
opportunity. So it's abou...
it's about giving the next...
developing world a brig...

Walter Bender, **Pre**...
Interview, 24 Apr 20...

What's new

Weekly current events · OLPC Planet · Current events archive

Deployments

- Teacher Training 🗗 **begins for** Bashuki and Bishwamitra **pilots**
- Nepal starts 🗗 **OLPC pilot program.**
- Laptop Training Begins in Peru 🗗
- **Waveplace starts pilot in** Port-Au-Prince, Haiti 🗗 **(video)**
- **The** Deployment Guide **is now posted to the wiki. Please help us improve it.**
- **Read about Nepal's upcoming deployments in** Bashuki Journal **and** Bishwamitra Journal
- **Astounded in Arahuay** 🗗 — Ivan Krstić on a followup visit to the site of Peru's 8-month OLPC pilot.
- The Inter-American Development Bank announced that it will finance a pilot project to test whether one-to-one computing can improve teaching and learning in schools in Haiti (the poorest country in the Western Hemisphere). The IDB will make a $3-million grant for the pilot project, which will distribute XO laptops to 13,200 students and 500 teachers in 60 Haitian primary schools. The OLPC Foundation will contribute XO laptops to the project through the Give One Get One program.
- **Read about OLPC in NYC on the** Teaching Matters 🗗 **blog.**
- Our Mongolia project **is the first deployment made possible by the generosity of the** Give One Get One **participants. Many than**... Mongolian children to those who contributed through the program.
- **So easy a child could do it** 🗗 — Birmingham 🗗 City School personnel attend OLPC workshop to learn about the XO
- IHT ran an AP article 🗗 on how the XO laptop and OLPC are transforming a remote Peruvian village

Search

Google search

Wiki search

About OLPC

- Home
- Community news
- Contact us
- Email lists and IRC
- Ways to participate

About the XO

- Help using the XO
- Support for the XO

Projects

- Educators
- Software
- Emulation
- Hardware
- Content
- Testing
- Peripherals
- Developers
- Deployment

OLPC wiki

- Recent changes
- Random page
- Help using the wiki

Toolbox

- What links here
- Related changes
- Upload file
- Special pages
- Printable version
- Permanent link

This website is a wiki for an organization. The site allows people to share information about this project.

Putting It Together

Research can be an exciting journey. Imagine you are one of the pupils researching animal testing. The subject might not be of interest to you. However, as you start your research, you come across information about cures for Alzheimer's disease. Your grandmother has Alzheimer's, and so this information interests you. You follow the research and soon find yourself in a section of the library with many books about Alzheimer's, people who had Alzheimer's, and experimental treatments. You start reading and taking notes. It is wonderful that you have found something fascinating. The problem is, this is not your research topic. No matter how interested you are in this new topic, you will still have to complete your project.

If this happens to you frequently, consider keeping a notebook in which you can write down ideas for future projects. This way you will not feel that you are being forced to ignore your interests. If you find that you are easily distracted, you will have to work at finding techniques to stay focused. Some people find that scheduling in breaks or only working for short periods can be helpful. You can also try to think of your topic from different angles. Perhaps your topic is anything to do with weather, and you are allowed to research any aspect of weather. You are not really interested in weather, but you do love computers. You could research the role computers play, and will play, in predicting and forecasting the weather. You've managed to stay on topic, but give it a focus that interests you more.

Imagine another scenario where you are reading about your assigned topic and, after an hour, you realize you have no idea what you just read. You do not understand the information, and so you are not interested in it. In both cases you need to step back for a minute and refocus yourself. There are several ways to do this, including taking a break, reading aloud, and taking notes. Other techniques are more specific.

Gathering information to answer your question can be overwhelming. It is helpful to decide in advance what type of information you need. There are several strategies that can be used to do this. One strategy is the use of a **KWL** chart (what I <u>K</u>now, what I <u>W</u>ant to know, and what I <u>L</u>earned). A KWL chart will help you connect what you already know about a topic with what you need to learn about it in order to answer your question or solve your problem.

KWL charts

You may already know a lot about a topic, from your previous experience. You may be only slightly familiar with other topics, and therefore only have a few facts about them. First decide what you already know about your subject. These facts will go in the first column of the KWL chart. Then determine what you still need to find out. These questions will go in the second column. When you have found enough facts to answer your question or solve your problem, you will fill in the last column of the chart.

Using this chart helps you to stay focused on what you need to learn as you do your research.

A sample KWL chart

Topic: Animal testing

Question: Should animals be used in medical testing?

What I **K**now	What I **W**ant to know	What I **L**earned
Some animal testing hurts animals.	Are there laws about animal testing?	Animal testing includes tests that do not harm animals.
Some animal testing creates drugs that save lives.	What are the economic issues?	The majority of people think there should be some limits on testing.
		Medical companies do not agree with the bans.

SQ3R

Another technique, known as **SQ3R**, can be very helpful when you are feeling disorganized. If the information you are reading seems overwhelming or unclear, taking a step back and looking at it in a new way can help you organise your thoughts. This technique is also useful when studying for exams or preparing presentations.

SQ3R stands for survey, question, and read, recite, and review (with "read, recite, and review" represented by "3R"). This is a technique that can only be used with print resources, such as books, magazines, or newspapers. The first step in using the SQ3R strategy is to look at the book jacket, the source title, the table of contents, the introduction to the source, the illustrations, and the **bibliography** and index. When surveying, you are quickly looking for the main points of the book's content. As you do it, you may develop questions related to your topic for which you would like further information. To answer the questions, you need to read carefully and take notes.

> ## Tips for being organised
>
> - Give yourself plenty of time – being in a rush leads to being disorganized.
> - Keep your materials in one place.
> - Make sure you have a clean, uncluttered work surface.
> - Keep careful notes of where you find information.
> - Create an order or system that makes sense for you – not all systems will work for everyone.
> - Try to avoid distractions, such as TV and surfing the Web for unrelated information.
> - Clear away your materials at the end of every work session.

In your notes you must use facts that are accurate, relevant, and complete. You need to be able to tell the difference between fact and opinion. You also need to determine the author's point of view or bias on a subject. Your notes will only contain the facts that are important for answering your question or solving your problem. Notes should not have long passages or sentences. They should have enough information to help you summarize your thoughts. In your notes, you should always include details of where you found the information. This will help you give proper credit later, and it will help if you have to find the information again. When you have finished taking notes, go back and reread the information, to make sure you have taken notes on all the important facts.

How to use SQ3R

Survey

- Survey the chapter, title, headings, subheadings, picture captions, charts, graphs, and maps.

- Survey the introduction and conclusion.

- Survey any further research questions and teacher-made study guides.

Question

- Turn the title, headings, and subheadings into questions.

- Read any questions at the ends of chapters.

- Ask yourself, "What did my teacher say about this chapter or subject?"

- Ask yourself, "What do I already know about this subject?"

Read

- Look for answers to the questions at the end of chapters or on a teacher-made study guide.

- Reread captions, charts, graphs, or maps.

- Note all the underlined, italicized, and bold-printed words or phrases.

- Reduce your speed for difficult passages.

- Stop and reread parts that are not clear.

- Read only a section at a time and recite after each section.

Recite

- Ask questions out loud about what you have just read.

- Take notes from the text, but summarize information in your own words.

- Underline or highlight important points you've just read.

- Recite answers out loud, remembering the more you see and hear your answers, the more likely you are to remember what you read.

Review

- Using your notes, mentally go over the material within 24 hours of reading it.

- Review again after a week.

- Review approximately once a month until your exam or presentation.

Organizing your sources

Once you have evaluated your information and know that you have as much as you need, you will have to organize it to write. Note cards can be very helpful for this. It is important to keep track of all of your sources, and creating one note card for each source is a good idea. These cards can later be helpful in writing your bibliography. A bibliography is a list of sources at the end of an essay or book that lists all the sources used in creating the work.

Keeping good source note cards will also help prevent you from accidentally committing **plagiarism**. Plagiarism is when you present someone else's words or ideas as your own. Keeping track of your sources as you read will also help you if you need to revisit a source to confirm information. Many people find it useful to keep a separate card for each fact they discover. It should also include where the information was found.

A - 1   page 4

Handyside, Christopher. <u>Jazz</u>.
      Heinemann Library, 2006.

Jazz music began in New Orleans, Louisiana,
as early as the 1890s.

A - 2   page 28

Handyside, Christopher. <u>Jazz</u>.
      Heinemann Library, 2006.

"Parker's playing style was more personal
and expressive than that of other
saxophonists. He seemed to be playing not
out of a need to entertain, but purely to
express himself."

Note cards can be helpful in organizing your research.

Paraphrasing and summarizing

On your note cards, you will probably have **paraphrases** and summaries. Paraphrases are restatements of information that you have put into your own words. A **summary** is a sentence that combines the information found in several sentences into one statement of fact. Direct quotations are statements taken directly from the source without changing any of the words. Direct quotations must begin and end with quotation marks to show they are not your words, but those of the author. You use direct quotations to provide support for the point of view being expressed in your presentation.

Citations

You will be using many sources as you find the answer to your research question or solution to your problem. Whatever information you include must be **cited**, or listed. Depending on what you are writing, the rules for how to cite sources will be different. Discuss with your teacher how he or she wants you to create a bibliography. As a general rule, bibliography entries will list the author, title, publication date, and publisher of the work. How to list these depends on the type of source (book, magazine, TV programme, website), as well as your topic.

Bibliography entries

Book
Author last name, first name. <u>Title of book</u>. Publisher, copyright date.

Magazine/Newspaper
Author last name, first name. "Title of article." <u>Title of magazine/newspaper</u>. Date: Page number(s).

Encyclopedia
Article author last name, first name. "Title of article." <u>Title of encyclopedia</u>. Volume. Publisher, copyright date.

Website
Author last name, first name. "Title of the article." <u>Title of the Web page</u>. Copyright date or revision date. Publisher of Web page. Day month year you saw the site. Web address.

Plagiarism

When you have found all your sources and done all your research, you will begin writing your essay. One thing you must be careful to avoid is plagiarism. Plagiarism is another word for cheating by copying. When you commit plagiarism, you submit someone else's ideas or words as your own.

Many people do this accidentally. They copy phrases or sentences from a book or article, forget where they found them, then copy them in their own essay. Other people incorrectly believe that if they have changed the words around, they have not committed plagiarism.

You wouldn't steal someone's belongings or answers in an exam, so why would you steal their thoughts?

40

How to avoid plagiarizing

Take careful notes:
- Make sure you take notes as you read. Write down where you read something and what page it was on.

- If you copy a quotation from a book, be sure to mark it as a quotation.

Give credit where credit is due:
- If you agree with something you read in book, you can use a phrase such as, "As Jane Austen says..." This lets the reader know who the thought belongs to.

- When writing your bibliography and footnotes, include more than is strictly necessary.

Use quotation marks:
- If you are quoting from a source, use quotation marks and make sure the sentence includes the information about where you read the quote.

Protect yourself:
- Be sure to give yourself enough time to complete your projects, that way you won't be tempted to take shortcuts.

- Keep drafts of your paper. Sometimes a pupil can be unfairly accused of plagiarizing. If you have copies of your notes and earlier drafts of your paper, you can prove that the thoughts are your own.

Catching plagiarism

Your teacher has many ways of discovering if you have copied from somewhere else. If your work does not seem to be written by you, he will become suspicious. If you have copied from another pupil, past or present, the teacher may recognize the work or ask other teachers if they recognize it. If you copy from a published source or something you find online, your teacher may type a few sentences into a search engine and discover that you have copied the work.

Most schools have strict rules against plagiarizing. The penalties can include you failing the project or exam, or even being suspended or expelled from school, even if your plagiarizing is accidental. Adults have lost their jobs and the respect of other people for committing plagiarism.

Some Reliable Sources

While each source should be evaluated for your individual needs, the following are some general categories and examples of reliable sources. Depending on your research topic, you may find other categories of reliable sources.

General category	Examples	Specific examples	Things to remember
Reference books and online sources	Encyclopedias Dictionaries Atlases Almanacs Websites for the above	*World Book Encyclopedia* *Oxford English Dictionary* *Times Atlas of the World*	Encyclopedias are usually only published every few years. The information in them may quickly become dated. Online versions of reference sources may be updated frequently. Libraries may have old copies of encyclopedias, dictionaries, and other reference sources. Check that the edition you find is the most recent one available.
Textbooks	Books you use in lessons		Textbooks are frequently updated, so make sure you are using the most current version, and that the book is recently published. Textbooks contain information on a lot of topics, so you may need to find more detailed information from other sources.

Websites	Company websites	www.kelloggs.com	These are websites run by companies. The main goal of the company is to sell you something.
			The information may be useful, especially if you are researching or comparing products.
	Educational websites	www.schoolhistory.co.uk	These are websites especially for school pupils. They are generally considered reliable sources of information.
	Government websites	www.defra.gov.uk	These are websites run by the government departments. They are generally considered reliable sources of information.
	Charity websites	www.unicef.org	These are websites run by not-for-profit organizations. They are generally considered reliable sources of information.
			These sites may belong to organizations that support particular causes, and so may show bias.
	Blogs	Blog.internationalpupil.com	A blog may be a website with personal opinions.
			Many companies run blogs. The company may try to hide the fact that they own the blog, to make the information seem more authentic.

Summary

In this book we have looked at ways of evaluating information. When you are looking for information to solve a problem or answer a question, you may find many sources with information you need. When conducting research, you will find some information that is factual, and some that expresses the opinions of the author. You need to be able to distinguish between fact and opinion, and know when to use each of them in answering your research question. Testing the relevance, completeness, and accuracy of the information will help you decide if this is information you can use to answer your research question or problem.

In researching your topic, you will consult many resources and read many facts. Some of the facts are related to, but not relevant to, your topic. Information must be significant to your topic to be used as a part of your answer. It is important to look for relevant information when researching your project.

Making decisions

As a researcher, you want to make sure the information you are using is accurate. Sometimes you will find information that contradicts other information you have found on the topic. When you find conflicting facts, verify which fact is correct by finding additional sources that give the same fact. Make sure the information is up-to-date by determining the age of the source. The Internet is an important source. As with other sources, you must determine who the author is for a website, and if they are qualified to write on the topic.

As you research your question, you may find inaccurate or misleading information. When researching, look at many sources. This will allow you to verify information from one source with information from other sources.

Gathering information to use to answer your question can be overwhelming. But by using strategies such as the 5 Ws, KWL charts, and SQ3R, you should be able to find relevant, accurate, and complete information that will answer your question or provide a solution to your problem.

Research is a learning process. You may not always get the answers you thought you would when you started, but if you take your work seriously, you will always learn something new.

When you know how to get the information
you need, research can be fun.

Glossary

bias   presenting information in a way that supports an opinion

bibliography   list that cites each source used in researching a topic

blog   abbreviation of the words "Web log". A site where entries are posted with the most recent first. Blogs are often a personal diary kept online.

cite   list as a reference

common knowledge   information that is known by a large number of people and is easily verifiable

copyright date   date that protection was given to an author or artist against copying in any form without the permission of the author or artist

database   collection of information that is stored on a computer or on a network accessible over the Internet

directory   Web page that contains links to selected websites on a variety of topics

domain name   part of a Web address that gives information about the type of website

hit   successful result of an Internet search

imprint page   page usually found at the front of a book listing publishing information

key word   word used in searching for information

KWL chart   table that helps to show what one **K**nows about a topic, what one **W**ants to know about the topic, and what one has **L**earned about the topic

objective   impartial, or not influenced by an opinion

opinion   information believed to be true based on some knowledge

paraphrase   restatement of a fact in one's own words

plagiarism   claiming someone else's words or thoughts as your own

rough draft   first attempt at writing an essay, usually improved upon and discarded

search engine   Web page that uses key words to search the Internet for websites

SQ3R   reading strategy used to understand what is being read. SQ3R means to Survey, Question, and Read, Recite, and Review.

summary   combining information into a shorter form

technical report   scientific report that describes the results of the study of a research topic

topic sentence   sentence that states the topic of a paragraph

URL   abbreviation for Uniform Resource Locator, which is the address of a website

verify   confirm as true

wiki   software that allows groups and individuals to create, edit, and link pages together

Find Out More

Books

The Study Skills Handbook, Stella Cottrell (Palgrave Macmillan, 2005)

How To Write Super School Reports, Elizabeth James and Carol Barkin (HarperTrophy, 1998)

Best Websites for Homework KS3, Andy Seed (Hodder, 2006)

Ready! Set! Research! Your Fast and Fun Guide to Research Skills That Rock!, Marvin Terban (Scholastic, 2008)

Websites

www.bized.co.uk/reference/studyskills/index.htm

This website is packed with information on study skills, covering many of the topics in this book and much more.

www.bbc.co.uk/schools/studentlife/revisionandskills

This part of the BBC website has helpful advice on many aspects of how best to carry out research.

www.virtualchase.com/quality/checklist.html
The Virtual Chase: How to Evaluate Information

Research

The best way to learn evaluation skills is to practise using them. Consider researching some of the topics discussed in this book, such as animal rights or global warming. Remember to evaluate information carefully.

Disclaimer

All the Internet addresses (URLs) given in this book were valid at the time of going to press. However, due to the dynamic nature of the Internet, some addresses may have changed, or sites may have changed or ceased to exist since publication. While the author and publishers regret any inconvenience this may cause readers, no responsibility for any such changes can be accepted by either the author or the publishers. It is recommended that adults supervise pupils on the Internet.

Index